Egon Schiele

© Confidential Concepts, worldwide, USA, 2004
© Sirrocco, London, 2004 (English version)

Published in 2004 by Grange Books
an imprint of Grange Books Plc
The Grange Kingsnorth Industrial Estate
Hoo, nr Rochester Kent ME3 9ND
www.Grangebooks.co.uk
ISBN 1-84013-655-3
Printed in China

Egon
Schiele

In 1964, Oskar Kokoschka evaluated the first great Schiele Exhibition in London as "pornographic". In the age of discovery of modern art and loss of "subject", Schiele responded that for him there exists no modernity, only the "eternal". Schiele's world shrank into portraits of the body, locally and temporally non-committal. Self-discovery becomes an unrelenting revelation of himself as well as of his models. The German art encyclopedia, Thieme and Becker, qualifies Schiele as an eroticist because Schiele's art represents the erotic portrayal of the human body. In this case, however, it is for him not only a study of feminine, but also male nudity. His models characterize an incredible freedom with respect to their own sexuality, self-love, homosexuality or voyeuristic attitudes, as well as skillful seduction of the viewer.

Clichés and criteria with regard to feminine beauty, perfect smoothness and sculpture-like coolness, however, do not interest him. He knows that the urge to look is interconnected with the mechanisms of disgust and allure. It is the body which contains the power of sex and death within itself. The photograph, *Schiele on his Deathbed* (p.8), depicts the twenty-eight year old nearly asleep, the gaunt body completely emaciated, head resting on his bent arm; the similarity to his drawings is astounding.

Because of the high danger of infection, the last visitors were able to communicate with the Spanish flu-infected Schiele only by way of a mirror, in which he viewed himself and his models, which was set up on the threshold between his room and the parlor.

During the same year, 1918, Schiele had designed a mausoleum for himself and his wife. Did he know, he who had so often distinguished himself as a person of sight, of his sudden end? Does individual fate fuse collectively with the fall of an old system here, that of the Habsburg Empire? Schiele's productive life scarcely extends beyond ten years, yet during this time he produced 334 oil paintings and 2,503 drawings (Jane Kallir, New York. 1990).

He painted portraits and still-life-like land and townscapes; however, he became famous as a draftsman. While Sigmund Freud exposes the repressed pleasure principles of upper-class Viennese society, which puts its women into corsets and bulging gowns and grants them solely a role as future mothers, Schiele bares his models. His nude studies penetrate brutally into the privacy of his models and finally confront the viewer with his own sexuality.

1. *The Scornful Woman (Gertrude Schiele)*, 1910. Gouache, watercolor and black crayon with white highlighting, 45 x 31.4 cm
Private collection

2. **Nude Girl with Folded Arms (Gertrude Schiele),** 1910. Watercolor and black crayon, 48.8 x 28 cm Graphische Sammlung Albertina, Vienna

3. **Seated Female Nude with Raised Right Arm**, 1910. Watercolor and black crayon, 45 x 31.5 cm Historisches Museum der Stadt Wien, Vienna

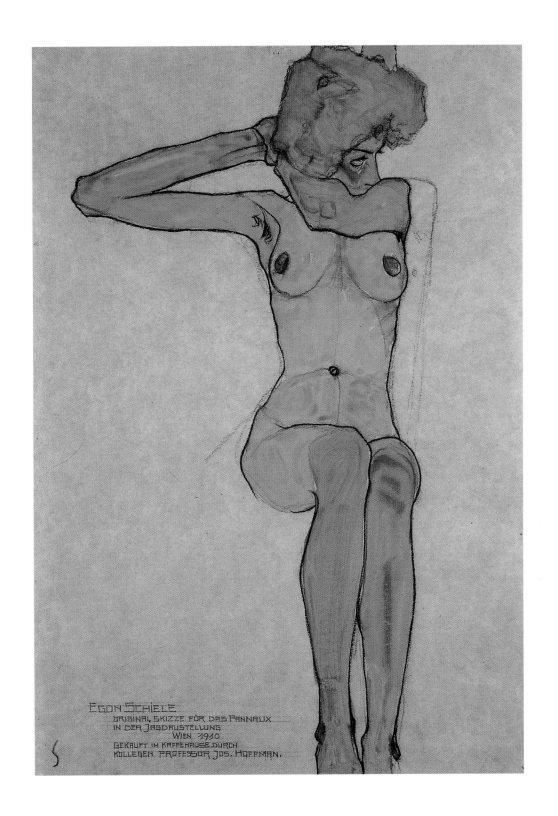

EGON SCHIELE
ORIGINAL SKIZZE FÜR DAS PANNAUX
IN DER JAGDAUSTELLUNG
WIEN 1910
GEKAUFT IM KAFFEEHAUSE DURCH
KOLLEGEN PROFESSOR JOS. HOFFMAN.

Schiele's Childhood

Under the sign of modern industrial times, with the noise of racing steam engines in factories and the human masses working there, Egon Schiele is born in the railway station hall of Tulln, a small, lower Austrian town on the Danube on June 12, 1890.

After his older sisters Melanie (1886-1974) and Elvira (1883-1893), he is the third child of the railway director Adolf Eugen (1850-1905) and his wife Marie, née Soukoup (1862-1935). The shadows of three male stillbirths are a precursor for the only boy, who in his third year of life will lose his ten-year-old sister Elvira.

The large infant mortality rate was the lot of former times, a fate which Schiele's later work and his picture of woman will characterize. In 1900, he attends the grammar school in Krems. But he is a poor pupil, who constantly takes refuge in his drawings, which his enraged father burns. In 1902, he sends his son to the regional grammar and upper secondary school in Klosterneuburg. The young Schiele has a difficult childhood marked by the illness of his father, who suffers from syphilis, which, according to family chronicles, he is said to have contracted while on his honeymoon as a result from a visit to a bordello in Triest.

9

His wife fled from the bedroom during the wedding night and the marriage was only consummated on the fourth day, on which he infected her also. Despair characterizes Schiele's father, who, retired early, sits at home dressed in his service uniform in a state of mental confusion. In the summer of 1904, stricken by increasing paralysis, he tries to throw himself out of the window.

Finally, he dies after grave suffering on New Year's Day 1905. The father, who during a fit of insanity burned all railroad stocks, leaves his wife and children destitute. The uncle, Leopold Czihaczek, chief inspector of the imperial and royal railway, assumes joint custody of the fifteen-year-old Egon, for whom he foresees the traditional family role of railroad man.

During this time, young Schiele wears the second-hand clothing of his uncle and fashions stiff white collars made from paper. It seemed that Schiele had been very close to his father for he, too, had possessed a certain talent for drawing, had collected butterflies and minerals and was very close to nature.

Years later, Schiele writes to his sister: "I have, in fact, experienced a beautiful spiritual occurrence today, I was awake, yet spellbound by a ghost who presented himself to me in a dream before waking, so long as he spoke with me, I was rigid and speechless." Unable to accept the death of his father, Schiele lets him rise again in visions.

He reports that his father had been with him and spoken much to him. In contrast, distance and misunderstanding characterize his relationship with his mother who, living in dire financial straits, expects her son to support her; in return, the older sister would work for the railroad.

6. *Female Nude*, 1910.
Gouache, watercolor and black crayon with white highlighting, 44.3 x 30.6 cm
Graphische Sammlung Albertina, Vienna

However, Schiele, who had been pampered by women during childhood, claims that "he is an eternal child". A wink of fate is the painter Karl Ludwig Strauch (1875-1959), who instructs the gifted youth in draftsmanship; the artist Max Kahrer of Klosterneuburg looks after the boy as well. In 1906, at the age of only sixteen, Schiele passes the entrance examination of the general art class at the Academy of Visual Arts in Vienna on his first attempt. Even the strict uncle, in whose household Schiele now takes his daily midday meal, sends a telegram to Schiele's mother: "Passed".

7. *Nude on Colored Fabric*, 1911.
Watercolor and pencil with white highlighting,
48 x 31 cm
Private collection

8. *One Contemplated in Dreams*, 1911.
Watercolor and pencil,
48 x 32 cm
The Metropolitan Museum of Art, New York

9. *Schiele, Drawing a Nude Model in Front of a* **Mirror**, 1910. Pencil, 55.2 x 35.3 cm Graphische Sammlung Albertina, Vienna

10. *Village with Mountains*, 1907. Oil on paper, 21.7 x 28 cm Private collection

15

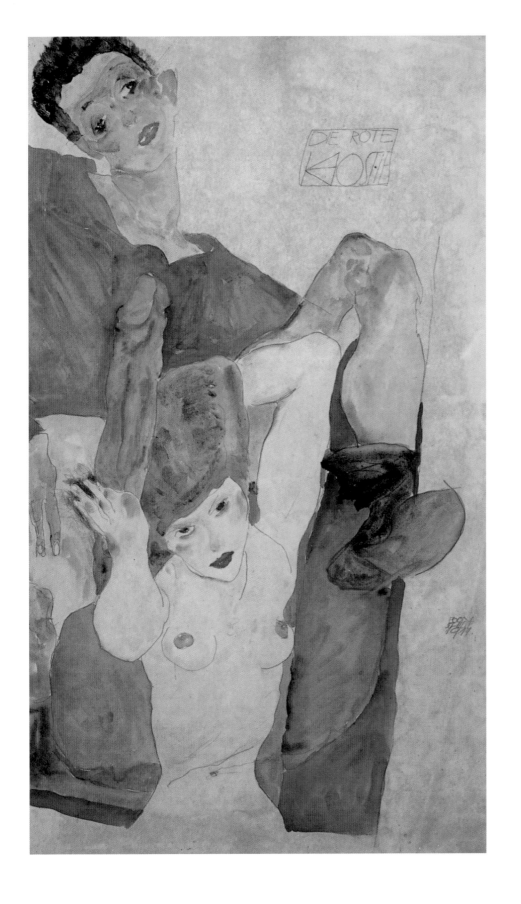

11. *Cardinal and Nun
 (Caress)*, 1912.
 Oil on canvas,
 69.8 x 80.1 cm
 Sammlung Rudolf
 Leopold, Vienna

12. *The Red Communion
 Wafer*, 1911.
 Watercolor and pencil,
 48.2 x 28.2 cm
 Private collection,
 courtesy of Gallery
 St. Etienne, New York

The Favorite Sister, Gerti

The nude study of the fiery redhead with the small belly, the fleshy bosom and the tousled pubic hair is his younger sister Gertrude (1894-1981) (p.2 and 4). In another watercolor, Gerti reclines backwards, still fully clothed with black stockings and shoes, and lifts the black hem of her dress from under which the red orifice of her body gapes. Schiele draws no bed, no chair, only the provocative gesture of his sister's body offering itself (p.9).

13. *Two Girls, Lying Entwined*, 1915. Gouache and pencil, 32.8 x 49.7 cm Graphische Sammlung Albertina, Vienna

Incestuous fantasies? The sister, four years his junior, is a compliant test object for him. At the time during which Sigmund Freud discovers that self-discovery occurs by way of erotic experiences, and the urge to look emerges as a spontaneous sexual expression within the child, young Egon records confrontation with the opposite sex on paper.

14. ***Two Girls Embracing (Friends)***, 1915.
Gouache, watercolor
and pencil,
48 x 32.7 cm
Szépmüvészeti
Múzeum, Budapest

He incorporates erotic games of discovery and a lively interest in the genitalia of his playmate into his nude studies. The forbidden gaze, searching for the opened female sheath beneath the rustling of the skirt hem and white lace. Gerti with her freckled skin, the green eyes and red hair is the prototype of all later women and models of Schiele.

Vienna at the Turn of the Century

Vienna is the capital city of the Danube monarchy, a state of multiple ethnicities consisting of twelve various nations with a population of approximately thirty million. Emperor Franz Josef maintains strict Spanish court etiquette. Yet, on the government's fortieth anniversary, he begins a large-scale conversion of the city with its approximately 850 public and private monumental structures and buildings. At this time, the influx of the rural population selling itself to the big city increases. Simultaneously, increasing industrialization results in the emergence of the proletariat in the suburbs, while the newly rich bourgeoisie settle in the exclusive Ring Street. In the writers' cafés, Leo Trotski, Lenin and later on Hitler consult periodicals on display and brood over the beginning century. Just how musty the artistic climate in Vienna was is evidenced in 1893 by the scandal over Engelhard's picture *Young Girl under a Cherry Tree*, which was repudiated on grounds of "respect for the genteel female audience, which one did not wish to embarrass so painfully vis-à-vis such an open-hearted naturalistic study". What mendacity, where official exhibitions of nude studies, the obligation of every artist, had long been an institution. In 1897, Klimt together with his Viennese fellow artists founded the Vienna Secession, a splinter group separated from the officially accepted conduct for artists under the motto: "To the times its art, to the art its freedom". In 1898, the first exhibition takes place in the building of the horticultural society. It is distinguished from the usual mass exhibitions of several thousand works in the sense that it offers an elite selection of 100 to 200 works of art. The proceeds generated by the attendance of the approximately 100,000 visitors finance the future exhibition building of the architect Olbrich. Exhibitions of Rodin, Kollwitz, Hodler, Manet, Monet, Renoir, Cézanne and van Gogh open the doors to the most up-to-date international art world. Visual artists work beside renowned writers and musicians such as Rilke, Schnitzler, Alternberg, Schönberg and Alban Berg for the periodical *Ver Sacrum*. Here they develop the idea of the complete work of art, which encompasses all artistic areas. Simultaneously, the Secession requires abolition of the distinction between higher and lower art, art for the rich and art for the poor and declares art common property. Yet, this demand of the art nouveau generation remains a privilege of the upper class striving for the ideal that "art is a life style", which encompasses architectural style, interior design, clothing and jewelry.

15. *The Dead Mother I*, 1910. Oil and pencil on wood, 32.4 x 25.8 cm Sammlung Rudolf Leopold, Vienna

16. ***The Dancer Moa***,
1911. Pencil,
watercolor and
gouache on paper,
47.8 x 31.5 cm
Leopold Museum
Privatstiftung, Vienna

17. ***Moa***, 1911.
Gouache, watercolor
and pencil,
48 x 31 cm Private
collection, on
extended loan to the
Museum of Modern
Art, New York

18. ***Wally in Red Blouse
with Raised Knees*,**
1913. Gouache,
watercolor and pencil,
31.8 x 48 cm
Private collection

19. ***Portrait of a Woman
(The Dancer Moa)*,**
1912. Pencil,
48.2 x 31.9 cm
Graphische
Sammlung Albertina,
Vienna

Gustav Klimt, the Father Figure

In 1907, Schiele makes the acquaintance of Gustav Klimt (1862-1918), who becomes his father figure and generously supports the talent of the young genius for the rest of his life. They exchange drawings with one another and Klimt even models for Schiele. In his career, Klimt profits from the large volume of commissioned work, such as the 24-meter-long Beethovenfries created for the faculty. Nevertheless, he runs into misunderstanding with the central motif of the embrace, a nude couple, with his contemporaries. Criticism against Klimt becomes more vehement with regard to his drawings for the simultaneously founded periodical *Ver Sacrum*, which was confiscated by a public prosecutor because "the depiction of the nude grossly violated modesty and, therefore, offended the public". Klimt answered that he wanted nothing to do with stubborn people.

20. ***Seated Male Nude (Self-Portrait)***, 1910.
    Oil and gouache,
    152.5 x 150 cm
    Sammlung Rudolf
    Leopold, Vienna

21. ***The Poet (Self-Portrait)***, 1911.
    Oil on canvas,
    80.1 x 79.7 cm
    Leopold Museum,
    Privatstiftung, Vienna

22. **Red Nude, Pregnant**,
1910. Watercolor and
charcoal,
44.5 x 31 cm
Private collection

23. **Newborn Baby**, 1910.
Watercolor and
charcoal, 46 x 32 cm
Private collection,
courtesy of Gallery
St. Etienne, New York

24. **Nude Self-Portrait**,
1910. Watercolor,
gouache and black
crayon with white
highlighting,
44.9 x 31.3 cm
Leopold Museum,
Privatstiftung, Vienna

What was decisive for him was who it was to please. For Klimt, who was supported by private patronage, this meant his clientele of Viennese middle-class patrons.

Schiele's Models

Contrary to Klimt, Schiele finds his models on the streets, young girls of the proletariat and prostitutes; he prefers the child-woman androgynous types. The thin, gaunt bodies of his models characterize lower-class status, while full-bosomed, luscious ladies of the bourgeoisie express theirs through well-fed corpulence. Yet, the attitude of the legendary Empress Sissi is symptomatic of a time in which the conventional picture of woman begins to sway. She indeed bears the desired offspring, however, rebels against the role of mother expected of her. The ideal of a youthful figure nearly causes her to become anorexic. At the same time, she shocks Viennese court society not only with her unconventional riding excursions, but also in that she wears her clothing without the prescribed stockings. During this time of the fin de siècle, Schiele portrays young girls from the working class. Vienna's number of prostitutes ranges among the highest per capita of any European city. Directly among the proletariat is where upper-class gentlemen found the defenseless objects of their desire, which they denied their own wives.

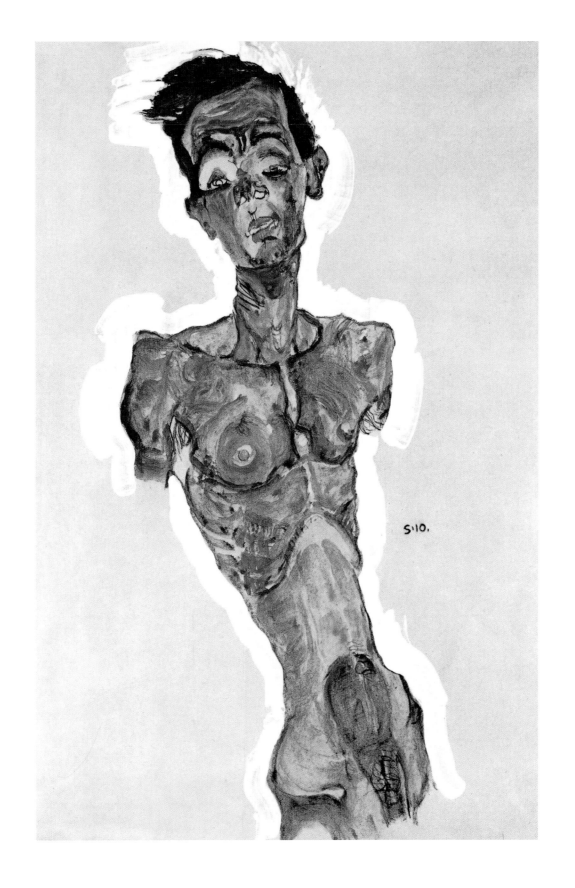

The young, gaunt bodies in Schiele's nude drawings almost stir pity; red blotches cover their thin skin and skeleton-like hands. Their bodies are tensed, however, the red genitalia are full and voracious. Like little animals, they lie in wait for the lustful gaze of the beholder. Despite their young age, Schiele's models are aware of their own erotic radiance and skillfully know how to set it into scene. The masturbating gesture of the hand on the vagina accompanies the provocative gaze of the model. Contrary to the hygienic taboos of the upper class, for example, not to linger overly long while washing the lower body or not to allow oneself to be viewed in the nude, Schiele's drawings testify to a simple body consciousness and the matter-of-course attitude with which the lower levels of society, where love for sale pertains to earning ones daily bread, deal with sexuality.

Outraged, the Viennese public lashes out at Schiele, stating that he paints the ultimate vice and utmost depravation, while he confronts both male and female spectators with their own, hypocritical sexuality. In a letter he writes: "Doing an awful lot of advertising with my prohibited drawings" and goes on to cite five notable newspapers which refer to him. Are his nude drawings but a sales strategy that help draw attention to himself? Klimt's picture of woman is based on the analogy of the female body as a personification of nature. Curled tresses become stylized plant formations and the wave-like silhouette melts into a consecrated atmosphere.

Schiele, however, breaks with the beautiful cult of organic art nouveau ornamental art. It is here, where Klimt offended the authorities in various episodes, namely in violating modesty, that Schiele finds his main objective. He radically bares persons of every decorative accessory and concentrates solely on their bodies. Yet, in contrast to the academic nude drawings, which mainly limit themselves to neutral coverage of the anatomy, Schiele brings the erotically-aroused body into play. He knows of the erogenous function that charms the eye and sets erotic signals with red painted lips, fleshy labia and dark moon circles under the eyes. The *One Contemplated in Dreams* opens her vulva (p.13).

Expressive Art Process

Drawings serve Klimt as preliminary studies for his paintings. In contrast, Schiele signs his watercolors as finalized works of art. It is precisely the sketch-like, unfinished product that characterizes Schiele, who unfolds the art process even in his oil paintings. In contrast to the ornamental surface art in art nouveau painting, his sharp line executions and jagged aggressive style suggest the artist's subjective guiding hand.

25. ***Black-Haired Nude Girl, Standing***, 1910. Watercolor and pencil with white highlighting, 54.3 x 30.7 cm Graphische Sammlung Albertina, Vienna

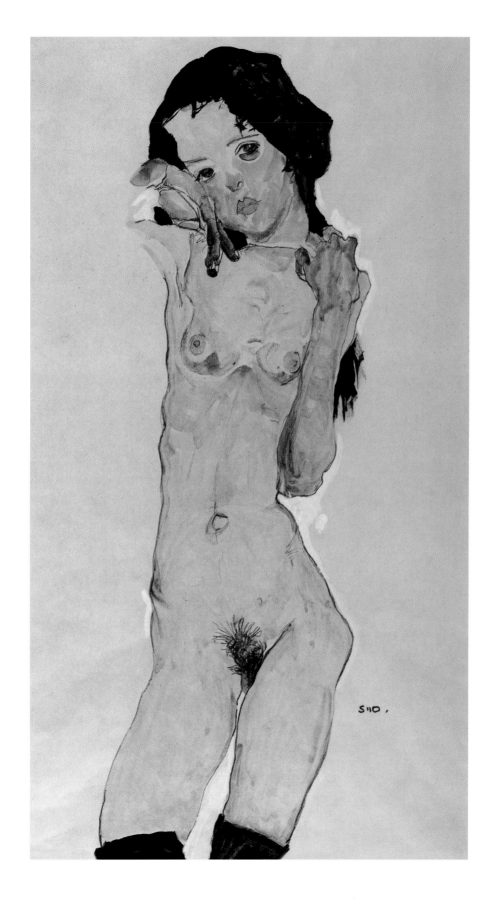

Encounter with the Mirrored Image

The contour line captures the physical presence and becomes a sculpture-like containment within space. Thereby Schiele dispenses with every spatiotemporal specification. Like a person regarding himself in a mirror, only seeing his face and body, like a lover who, within the body of his love, forgets the world around him, Schiele creates his self-portraits before a mirror, as well as some of his female nude drawings. *Schiele, Drawing a Nude Model in Front of a Mirror* illustrates this (p. 14). The scene is very illuminating, the duplication of frontal and rear views of the nude woman are revealed in the reflection, however, there, where the mirror is, stands the viewer. He functions as the mirror in which the model regards herself, reassuring herself of her body, and in whose gaze it moves. The intimacy between painter and model is countered in relationship to viewer and drawing.

First Exhibitions

In 1908, Schiele partakes in a public exhibition in the imperial hall of the Klosterneuburg Monastery for the first time. Subjects are the small-scale landscapes which he had painted out-of-doors from summer through to the fall (p.15). According to Jane Kallir, around the end of 1908, Schiele had painted nearly half of all the oil paintings of his lifetime.

"New Artists"

It was only in 1909 that Schiele's artistic creativity reached the great turning point. He leaves the academy, in particular the reactionary professor Christian Griepenkerl, and establishes together with Anton Peschka, Albert Paris von Gütersloh, Anton Faistauer, Sebastian Isepp and Franz Wiegele and others the "New Art Group" (Neukunstgruppe). The formula of the new artists is opposition. Schiele's retreat from the subjective experience of the individual is the counter reaction to Viennese historicism and its prince of painters, Hans Makart, celebrated by the government. Schiele distances himself from their allegoric similes; the pompous veils fall. He turns Catholicism's conventional concepts of value upside down and places them into the service of sexuality. His strategy: he wants to shock. In the painting provocatively titled *The Red Communion Wafer* (p.17), Schiele reclines on his back in an orange shirt with his abdomen bared, his spread legs suggesting the feminine gesture of submission, while before him, gazing at the viewer, a nude strawberry-blonde holds the enormous phallus. In other paintings, monks make love to nuns and expectant women who were often unwelcome and repudiated by strict Viennese society (p.16).

26. ***Portrait of Friederike Maria Beer***, 1914.
Oil on canvas,
190 x 120.5 cm
Private collection

27. ***Woman with Black Stockings***, 1913.
Gouache, watercolor
and pencil,
48.3 x 31.8 cm
Private collection,
courtesy of Gallery
St. Etienne, New York

"The nun prays chafed and nude before *Christ's Agony on the Cross*" (Georg Trakl, Munich, 1974). Furthermore, Schiele paints homosexual couples, transgresses taboos and provokes the fantasies of his contemporary viewers. In turn, Schiele finds acknowledgement at the international art show in Vienna where he is represented by four paintings next to the expressionist works of Vincent van Gogh, Edvard Munch and Oskar Kokoschka. He makes the acquaintance of Josef Hoffman, the director of the Vienna workshop. In December of 1909, the first exhibition of the "New Art Group" takes place at the Pisko's fine art dealership.

Vienna Art Scene

In 1909, thus relatively early, Schiele makes the acquaintance of decisive personalities of the Vienna art scene, whose portraits he painted and who were to remain loyal to him for his entire life and beyond. Schiele makes the acquaintance of Arthur Roessler, writer and art critic, who becomes one of the most decisive friends and promoters of Schiele. Further figures influencing his career are publisher Eduard Kosmack, the publisher of the magazines *The Architect* and *The Interior*, Carl Reininghausen (1857-1929), who was one of the most important Viennese collectors and the railroad official and Schiele collector Heinrich Benesch (1862-1947), who later dedicated a book to Schiele.

Schiele's Close Circle of Friends

Perhaps because Schiele opposes the plans of his uncle, who would like to persuade his ward to enter military service, Czihaczec withdraws his guardianship in 1910. During the same period, the incident with the mysterious lover occurs, of which, with the exception of an exchange of letters with the gynecologist Erwin von Graff who assures Schiele that he has admitted her to his clinic and is attending to her, nothing is known. Schiele deals with this incident in several paintings: *Birth of the Genius* and *The Dead Mother* (p.21). He paints a fetus, which, still in the womb of the mother, stares at the beholder. During this time, love and death studies go hand-in-hand. On the one hand, the sexual act is associated with the danger of pregnancy and the possible verdict of having to die while in the childbed, where the life-bestowing body is desecrated to death. On the other, syphilis lurks in every kiss. Is it possible to explain the subliminal, morbid trait in Schiele's world of man herewith? The significance of woman in turn is limited solely to her biological function of childbearing in the cult book of that time by the author Otto Weininger *Sex and Character*, who comments that men of significance should only get involved with prostitutes.

28. ***Crouching Nude in Shoes and Dark Stockings, Back View***, 1912. Gouache, watercolor and pencil on paper, 48.9 x 32 cm The Metropolitan Museum of Art, New York, Bequest of Scotfield Thayer, 1982

Whereas Freud discovers: "Upbringing denies women the intellectual occupation with sex problems, wherefore, nevertheless, they bring with them the greatest desire for knowledge; startles them with the condemnation, that desiring such knowledge is unfeminine and a sign of a sinful predisposition. Thus, they are deterred from thinking at all, knowledge is devalued for them." Inasmuch, Freud attributes alleged intellectual inferiority of so many women to sexual repression, which results in inhibition of thought.

Accompanied by his friend, the painter and mime Erwin Osen, Schiele flees to Krumau where they spend the summer with a dancer named Moa (p.22 and 23), the lover of Osen. Here Schiele also makes the acquaintance of the young baccalaureate Willy Lidl, who avows his deep love for him. Back in Vienna, Schiele shares his atelier with Max Oppenheimer (1885-1954). Day in, day out, he lives from hand to mouth. Even if young Schiele laments of financial woes, he quickly manages to get on his feet again and finds support from friends and patrons.

Then in 1910, Vienna workshops, established in 1903, print three of Schiele's picture cards; at the same time he is represented with a painting at the international hunters exhibition in the context of the Klimt group. A further exhibition at the Klosterneuburg monastery exhibits the portrait of Eduard Kosmack and that of a boy, Rainerbub, son of the Viennese orthopedist and surgeon Max Rainer (1910). As early as 1911, the first monograph on Schiele, penned by the artist and poet Albert Paris von Gütersloh, is published. In the same year, Arthur Roessler reviews Schiele's works in the monthly periodical *Bildende Künstler*. In Vienna, Schiele partakes in the collective exhibition of the Miethke Gallery.

Wally, the First Life's Companion

Once again, Schiele wants to get away. "Vienna is full of shadows, the city is black. I want to be alone (in)to the Bohemian Woods, that I need not hear anything about myself," he writes in his diary. Wally, (Valerie) Neuzil, former model and lover of Klimt, who supposedly gave her to Schiele, accompanies him. They move to his mother's home town in Krumau on the Moldau. The devoted Lidl had procured the atelier with the garden. A very productive working phase begins for Schiele. Besides a few landscapes, he mainly works on nude studies of himself and Wally, his "twittering lark" (p.24). Like the diary drawings, numerous studies cover the erotic cohabitation of two bodies.

29. *Three Girls*, 1911.
Watercolor and pencil,
48 x 31.5 cm
Private collection

30. *Seated Nude Girl,*
   1910. Gouache and
   black crayon with
   white highlighting,
   44.8 x 29.9 cm
   Graphische
   Sammlung Albertina,
   Vienna

31. ***Two Girls on Fringed Blanket***, 1911.
Gouache, watercolor,
ink and pencil,
56 x 36.6 cm
Private collection,
courtesy of Gallery
St. Etienne, New York

32. ***Hindering the Artist is a Crime, it is Murdering Life in Bud!***, 1912.
Watercolor and pencil, 48.6 x 31.8 cm
Graphische Sammlung Albertina, Vienna

Self-Portrait as Nude Study

There are approximately 100 self-portraits with several nude studies of Schiele (p.26). Illustration of masculine nude studies is obligatory at the academy, psychologized self-depiction, however, apart from Richard Gerstl in 1908, is the exception.

The self-portrait as nude study positions the artist not only as a person of sight, but also in his physical being. Schiele does not act as voyeur in baring his models, rather, he brings himself into play.

The nude study depicting the rigid member, masturbating, goes a step further and depicts him as the man fascinated by his own sexuality (p.27). In the urge to look and show, voyeur and exhibitionist, Freud differentiates between a look directed at an unfamiliar object and turning the body on show against a part of one's own body.

This reversal in passivity accompanies the setting of a new goal: to be looked at. The urge to look is indeed autoerotic from the beginning; it surely has an object but finds it in the own body. In turn, the showing of the genitals is well known as an apotropaic action. Accordingly, Freud interprets "the showing of the penis and all its surrogates" as the following statement: "I am not afraid of you, I defy you."

Schiele, the Man of Pain

The discrepancy between Schiele's external appearance and his repulsively ugly self-portraits is astonishing (p.29). Gütersloh describes Schiele as "exceptionally handsome", of well-maintained appearance, "someone who never had even a day-old beard", an elegant young man, whose good manners strangely contrasted his reputedly unpalatable manner of painting.

Schiele, on the other hand, paints himself with a long high forehead, wide opened eyes deep in their sockets and tortured expression, an emaciated body, which he sometimes mutilates up to its trunk, with spider-like limbs. The bony hands tell of death at work. His body reflects the sallow colors of decay.

In many places, he paints himself with a skull-like face. Schiele admits in a verse: "everything is living dead". Just as Kokoschka maintains, Schiele soliloquizes with death, his counterpart. "And surrounded by the flattery of decay, he lowers his infected lids" (Georg Trakl, Munich, 1974).

33. *Egon Schiele, 1914.*
Photograph by Anton Josef Trcka, Graphische Sammlung Albertina, Vienna

34. *Standing Girl in Blue Dress and Green Stockings, Back View*, 1913. Watercolor and pencil, 47 x 31 cm Private collection

At the same time, Schiele perceives himself as a man of pain: "That I am true I only say, because I ... sacrifice myself and must live a martyr-like existence." If contemporary art banished religious themes from its field of vision, the artist now incarnates these himself.

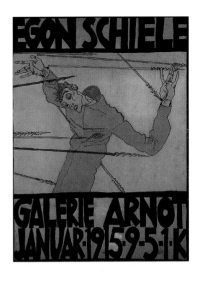

In a letter to Roessler the Christ-likeness becomes clearer still: "I sacrificed for others, for those on whom I took pity, those who were far away or did not see me, the seer." His fate as an outsider leads to the ideal of the artist as world redeemer. In the program of the New Artists he explains: "Fellow men feel their results, today in exhibitions. The exhibition is indispensable today ... the great experience in the existence of the artist's individuality." For him, however, this no longer concerns telling illustration, rather, representation of his soul's inner life. The nude study is a revealing study. Thereby, the work in its expressive self-staging becomes a performative study of his life.

Fascination with Death

Viennese of the turn of the century live with a longing for death and romanticize the "beautiful corpse". "How ill everything coming into being does seem to be," writes Trakl, who in 1914 finds death at the front. Schiele shares with Osen, who has himself locked away in a Steinhof insane asylum where he might study the mimic of patients there, the interest for pathologic pictures of disease. In the clinic of the gynecologist Erwin von Graf, he studies and draws sick and pregnant women and pictures of new and stillborn infants (p.28).

Schiele is "fascinated by the devastation of foul suffering, to which these, in principal innocents, are exposed. Astonished, he saw unusual changes in the skin, in whose sagging vessels thin, watery blood and tainted fluids trickled sluggishly, he marveled also at light-sensitive green eyes behind red lids, the slimy mouths and the soul in these unsound vessels," reports Roesseler.

Therein he resembles Oskar Kokoschka, called the "soul slasher" and of whom it was said that "painting hand and head, he lay bare in ghostly manner the spiritual skeleton of her whom he portrayed". To the color lithograph of his drama, *Murder Hope of Women*, he comments: "The man is bloody red, the color of life, but he lies dead in the lap of a woman, who is white, the color of death." Man and woman form the dance of life and death.

35. *Self-Portrait as St. Sebastian (Poster)*, 1914-1915. Gouache, black crayon and ink on cardboard, 67 x 50 cm Historisches Museum der Stadt Wien, Vienna

36. *Coitus*, 1915.
Gouache and pencil,
31.6 x 49.8 cm
Leopold Museum,
Privatstiftung, Vienna

Phantom-Like Creatures

With a few lines, Schiele sketches the outlines of the body on paper. A thigh is reduced to two lines. The stroke is dynamic, grows fainter, following the structural ductility of a fast thrown-in movement. Jagged, with hard angles he loves the bone structure.

Schiele's stroke becomes calligraphy, which captures the body's expression with just a few lines. Yet, in contrast to the reluctant, bony aspect of the shoulders and pelvis is the round diffraction of the chest, orange nipples and vulva become wounds.

37. *Sitting Woman with Bent Leg*, 1917.
Gouache, watercolor and black crayon, 46 x 30.5 cm
Národni Gallery, Prague

The physiognomy of his models, however, remains anonymously phantom-like, the button eyes could sooner belong to a doll, which could be any woman. The body posture is directed at the gaze of the viewer, before whom she exhibits her genitals. Peculiar, however, is the splayed gesture of the hands; these appear intractably hard and therein call to mind the hands of Schiele.

Body Perspectives

Schiele ignores light and shadow effects which model the body, dispenses with shadow strokes and divests the character of all spatial containment. In his atelier, he often works on a ladder, from where he captures his models from a bird's eye view perspective in an extreme visual angle of under and oversight.

This calls to mind one of his verses: "An intimate bird sits in a leafy tree, he is dull colored, hardly moves and does not sing; his eyes reflect a thousand greens." He isolates his creatures in his view, sets them into a world without time or place. Bodies form space.

Exemplary of the spatial lack of orientation of his characters is the commissioned artwork for Friederike Maria Beer, the fashion conscious daughter of a cabaret proprietor who actively followed Viennese art events (p.33).

38. *Reclining Female Nude*, 1917. Gouache, watercolor and charcoal, 29.7 x 46.3 cm Moravská Galéri, Brno

On Schiele's suggestion, she allows her full body likeness to be painted on the ceiling. It shows her in a variegated dress with mime-like bearing, her body strangely floating, free of all gravitational pull, raised arms with the indefinable hand gesture call to mind Schiele's self-portraits once again.

Vampire-Like Trait of the Sex

Ulrich Brendel writes in the periodical *Die Aktion* that Schiele is said to capture "the vampire-like trait of the sex". His models lament: "It is no pleasure; he always sees only the one thing." At the same time, Freud discovers the fear of castration mechanism: "the sight of Medusa's head, that is to say, that of the feminine genitalia, causes one to become rigid with fright, transforms the beholder into stone. Because to become rigid signifies the erection." A girl, her face remaining anonymously sketch-like, reclines backwards; her uplifted skirt is a work of pleats out of which her genitals peek becoming an inner eye slit. Again and ever again, Schiele discovers and sees, shows and offers the most intimate, forbidden part to the viewer. He carefully watercolors it into a full fruit, a calyx of orange color.

39. ***Seated Woman in Violet Stockings***, 1917. Gouache and black crayon, 29.6 x 44.2 cm Private collection

40. ***Portrait of the Artist's Wife Seated, Holding Her Right Leg***, 1917. Gouache and black crayon, 46.3 x 29.2 cm The Pierpont Morgan Library, New York

Disgust and Allure

Schiele scarcely models the bodies he paints, only a few colored splotches animate the white paper surface on which the body seems to lie confined by a few lines. Schiele's patron, Carl Reininghausen, whom Schiele instructs in drawing and painting, complains that he "paints so casually that the composition is no longer recognizable in places due to the splotches". The marks on the body executed by the use of a wash cause astonishment; often in contrasting colors of green and red, they create aggressive tension. In contrast to the general impression of the shape, the splotches point to the closer view, this intimacy with everything else exposes the condition of the skin. Schiele's models do not possess unblemished white, alabaster bodies, rather, he gets under their skin. "The body becomes a wound." (Werner Hofmann, Munich, 1981) Schiele turns the fleshy inner part of the vagina inside out.

41. ***Death and the Maiden***, 1915-1916. Oil on canvas, 150 x 180 cm Österreichische Galerie, Belvedere, Vienna

42. ***Seated Couple (Egon and Edith Schiele)***, 1915. Pencil and gouache on paper, 52.5 x 41.2 cm Graphische Sammlung Albertina, Vienna

As to the aesthetics of the color splotches, which, like the famous splotched paintings by Rorschach, render the viewer a projection surface, Hugo von Hofmannstal reminds that "art is magical writing, which uses colored splotches instead of words to portray an internal vision of the world, a puzzling one, without being". Contemporaries, however, characterize Schiele's art as "manically demonic".

"Some of his pictures are the materializations of obscured consciousness of apparitions grown bright." His friend Roessler in turn stresses that his face is the synthesis of inner human existence.

Doubtless, the nude studies reflect the inner world of the soul's condition imposed onto the model by the artist. "I am everything at once, but never shall I do everything all at once," declared Schiele, who multiplicates through psychological role-playing and fuses into the picture of his models. Thereby, all artistic means aim at capturing the psychological experience of Schiele himself.

The Age of the Pornographic Industry

In the year 1850, with the invention of photography, in particular the daguerreotype, pornographic photos also come into fashion. On the one hand, the photos served as a model for artists, also for Schiele, who made quite a few photos of his models. On the other hand, they were collector items for erotomanics.

Mainly, however, they were used as presentation cards at bordellos by means of which the visitor could compile his "menu". The production of erotic pictures was not prohibited, advertising was. In so doing, the models as well as the photographer risked going to jail.

The first conviction follows in 1851. When 4,000 obscene prints and four large albums of "nude women" are discovered in the possession of the French photographer Joseph-Antoine Belloc, he receives a minor sentence of three months detention.

The models were largely prostitutes, easy women, but also working women in dire financial straits and gutter children picked up from the streets. To satisfy voyeuristic desire, the Munich publisher Guilleminot Recknagel had a stock of 4,000 photos of ten to thirty-year-old models. Starting in approximately 1870, erotic postcards came into circulation.

43. *Standing Nude Girl*, 1918. Black crayon on paper, 45.7 x 29.5 cm, Private collection, New York

Thematic scenes of Greek and Roman mythology, heroic or Christian martyr scenes with the naked Magdalene, crucifixion of female characters and nude Greeks were to give these photos a certain value. In provisional theaters, such adjustment of pictures is very popular.

44. *Cover of the Egon Schiele issue of Die Aktion*, 1916. Graphische Sammlung Albertina, Vienna

45. *Reclining Woman*, 1917. Oil on canvas, 95.5 x 171 cm Sammlung Rudolf Leopold, Vienna

46. *The Family (Squatting Couple)*, 1918. Oil on canvas, 152.5 x 162.5 cm Österreichische Galerie Belvedere, Vienna

Famous collectors were the Marquis of Byros in Vienna and in Munich Doctor Kraft Ebbing. Particularly the Baron von Meyer loved the "sweet girls" from Vienna. Schiele surely profited from the high sales of pornographic photos in direct relation to lustful consumption. Yet, his erotic drawings testify to a personal question which in turn is embodied in the epoch of decadence, namely the dialectics of carnal desire and death instinct.

Schiele's Arrest

In August 1911, Schiele feels impelled to relocate to Neulengbach near Vienna in Lower Austria with Wally. His retreat to the country was naïve and out of touch with reality. Inevitably, he would offend the conservative population with his unorthodox life style.

Predictably, living in sin with the still under-age Wally would rile the population of the provincial town against Schiele. For the village youth, however, Schiele's studio was a haven of well being.

47. *Embrace (Lovers II)*,
1917. Oil on canvas,
100 x 170.2 cm
Österreichische
Galerie, Belvedere,
Vienna

Gütersloh describes the free-spirited atmosphere: "well, they slept, recuperated from parental thrashings, lazily lolled about, something they were not permitted to do at home"; until April 13, 1912, when a catastrophic incident came about.

The father of a thirteen-year-old girl, who had run away from home and found refuge in Schiele's home, reported him for kidnapping. The charge is withdrawn, but Schiele is arrested and charged with endangering public morality and circulation of "indecent" drawings. Schiele's defense by Heinrich Benesch, however, is naïve, when he writes: "Schiele's carelessness is responsible for the incident. Whole swarms of little boys and girls came into Schiele's studio to frolic.

There they saw the nude study of a young girl." For the sake of his art, Schiele forgets all modesty, lifts the skirts of the sleeping children, surprises two girls embracing one another.

48. ***Portrait of the Artist's Wife, Seated***, 1918.
Oil on canvas,
139.5 x 109.2 cm
Österreichische
Galerie, Belvedere,
Vienna

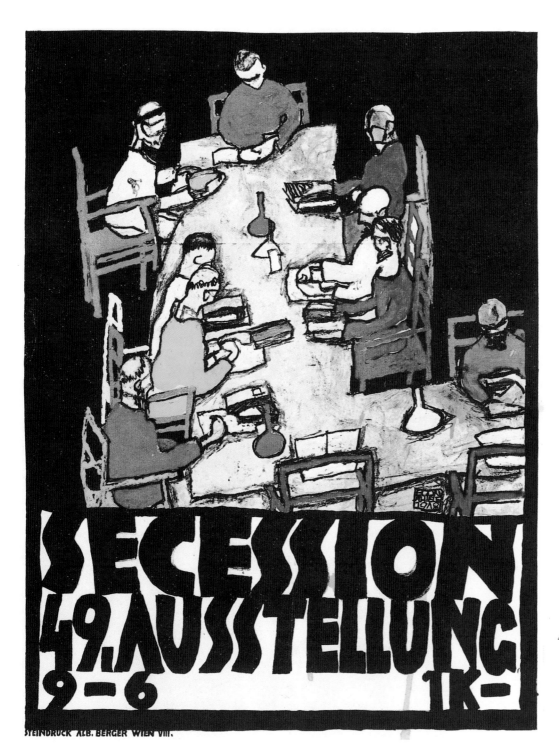

49. *Poster for the 49th Secession Exhibition*, 1918. Lithograph, 63.5 x 48 cm Graphische Sammlung Albertina, Vienna

50. ***Prophets (Double Self-Portrait)***, 1911.
Oil on canvas,
110.3 x 45.3 cm
Staatsgalerie Stuttgart

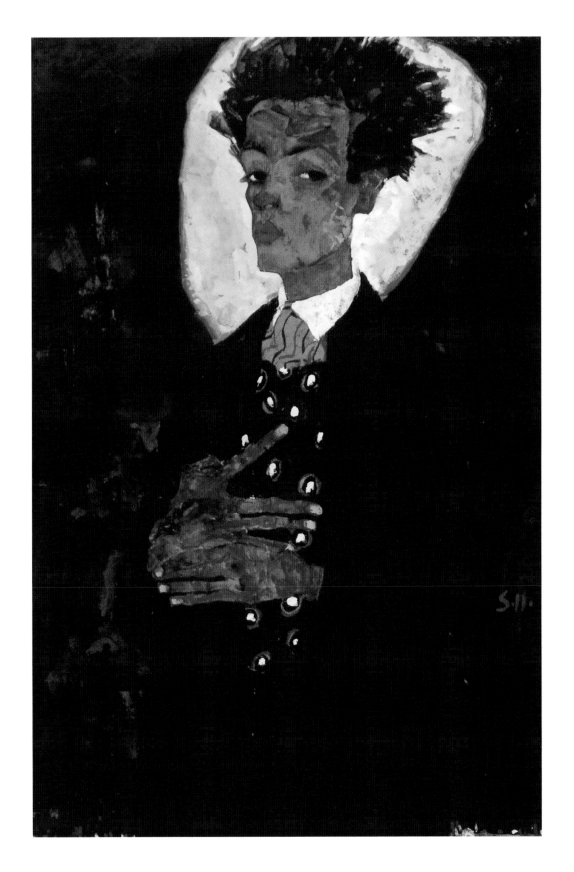

51. ***Self-Portrait with a Peacock Cardigan***, 1911. Watercolor, gouache, aquarelle and oil pencil on paper on cardboard, 51.5 x 34.5 cm

Exposure of his own private sphere as well as that of others becomes a confession-like, artistic expression of his own truthfulness. The private sphere and public domain become interchangeable.

Schiele's influential collector Carl Reininghausen procures an attorney in Vienna for him, but at the same time dispenses with the "cordial you" (informal) between them. In St. Pölten, Schiele spends 24 days in custody. He pleads: "To inhibit an artist is a crime. It is called murder of life coming into being" (p.40).

The prison stay validates him, the artist, in his role as an outsider. "The one orange was the only light." Several self-portraits of Schiele as prisoner testify to this time. Solemnly the judge will burn one of the indecent drawings in the courtroom. There then Schiele expresses: "I do not feel chastised, but cleansed."

International Artist

In Munich the art dealer Golz exhibits Schiele's works. In this critical year of 1912, the "New Art Group", together with the artists union, displays *Der Blaue Reiter* (The Blue Rider) in Budapest, Munich and Essen.

In November 1912, Schiele returns to Vienna and moves into an atelier in the Hiertzinger Hauptstrasse. Klimt acquaints him with the collector August Lederer, whose son Erich becomes his pupil. Franz Pfemfert publishes poems and drawings by Schiele in the Berlin periodical *Die Aktion*.

Three of Schiele's works can be seen in the international special alliance exhibition in Cologne. The lithograph *Male Nude Study* appears in the Sema-Mappe (portfolio) of the Delphin Publishing House in Munich.

In 1913, Schiele becomes a member of the Bund österreichischer Künstler (federation of Austrian artists), of which Gustav Klimt is president. In the same year, he goes to Munich, where he partakes in the collective exhibition of the Galerie Golz.

52. *Preacher*, 1913.
Gouache, watercolor
and lead,
47 x 30.8 cm
Rudolf Leopold
Collection, Vienna

On July 28, 1914, war is officially declared between the Austro-Hungarian Empire and Serbia. Schiele comments: "We live in the most violent time the world has ever seen. Hundreds of thousands of people perish miserably, everyone must bear his fate either living or dying; we have become hard and fearless.

53. ***Self-Portrait Arms Drawn-Back***, 1915.
Gouache, pastel and charcoal,
32.9 x 44.8 cm
Private collection

54. ***Two Little Girls***,
1911. Gouache,
watercolor and lead,
40 x 36 cm
Graphische
Sammlung Albertina,
Vienna

That which was before 1914 belongs to another world." Schiele continues with his work, he is now an internationally recognized artist, who partakes in exhibitions in Rome, Brussels and Paris. Anton Josef Trcka (1893-1940) photographs Schiele in extravagant pantomime poses, in a strong gesticulating blind language (p. 41).

In the Berlin periodical *Die Aktion* he writes: "We are above all people of the times, in other words, such who have at the very least found the way into our present time." In 1915, the Vienna Galerie Arnot dedicates an exclusive exhibition of sixteen paintings, watercolors and drawings to Schiele, among them, Schiele's *Self-Portrait as St. Sebastian* (p. 43).

With this religiously engaged role model, he stands in the tradition of Oskar Kokoschka, Rainer Maria Rilke and Georg Trakl, who see themselves as martyrs tormented by society, yet at the same time, Schiele holds the reins of his career adroitly in hand.

55. *Mother and Child*,
1910. Gouache,
watercolor and lead,
55.6 x 36.5 cm
Historisches Museum,
Vienna

56. *Seated Little Girl*,
1911. Watercolor and
lead, 46.5 x 31.8 cm
Bayerische
Staatsgemäldesamm-
lungen, Munich

57. ***Group of Three Girls***,
    1911. Gouache,
    watercolor and lead
    with white brights,
    44.4 x 30.8 cm
    Graphische
    Sammlung Albertina,
    Vienna

58. ***Pregnant Woman and
    Dead Man***, 1911.
    Oil on canvas,
    100.3 x 100 cm
    Narodni Galerie,
    Prague

Schiele's Skillful Social Maneuver

Schiele's beloved sister Gerti marries a fellow artist, Anton Peschka, whose young son often spends time with his uncle. Across from Schiele's atelier lived his landlords, the middle-class Harms family with their two young daughters.

Schiele, disguised as an Apache, allows them to see him at the window. Later he sends Wally with an invitation to the cinema and the assurance that she too would accompany them. The two sisters model for Schiele and, in their vanity, compete for the favors of the young artist.

Coldheartedly he informs Wally that he will marry Edith (p.49), the socially advantageous match for him, whereupon she joins the Red Cross as a nurse and goes to the front where she will succumb to scarlet fever in 1917.

In the allegorical painting *Death and the Maiden* Schiele himself comes to terms with his separation from Wally (p.50).

The Bourgeois Schiele

On June 17, 1915, five days after his twenty-fifth birthday, Schiele marries Edith Harms. Four days later, he is inducted into military service in Bohemia.

In 1916, he is held captive in the Russian prisoner of war camp located in Mühlung near Wieselburg. *Die Aktion* publishes two xylographs. One year later, Schiele returns to Vienna to work in the army museum. In the beginning, his wife is his exclusive model.

However, as she grows plumper, Schiele once again begins to look for models elsewhere. In 1918, 117 sessions with other models are recorded in his notebook.

The Vienna book dealer Richard Lanyi publishes a portfolio with twelve collotypes of Egon Schiele's drawings.

59. ***Death Pangs***, 1912.
Oil on canvas,
70 x 80 cm
Bayerische
Staatsgemälde-
sammlungen, Munich

In December, Schiele works for the periodical *The Dawn*. In a letter of March 2, 1917, Schiele writes to his brother-in-law: "Since the bloody terror of world war befell us, some will probably have become aware that art is more than just a matter of middle-class luxury."

60. *Otto Wagner Portrait*,
1910. Watercolor and
lead with white
brights, 43.5 x 26 cm
Historisches Museum
der Stadt Wien,
Vienna

Schiele, a Celebrated Artist

After the sudden death of Klimt and the exile of Kokoschka, Schiele is the celebrated artist in Vienna. Very successfully, he partakes in the 49th Vienna Secession of 1918 with 19 large paintings and 24 drawings. Franz Martin Haberditzl purchases the *Portrait of the Artist's Wife, Seated* for the Moderne Galerie. It is the first acquisition of a painting while the artist is yet alive. However, Schiele must paint over the plaid skirt, as the museum's director finds it too indecent (p.58). Schiele can now afford a larger atelier, the old one is to become an art school. Already in 1917, Schiele had a plan for an art center, where the various disciplines of literature, music and visual art coexist.

The best-known founding members are Schönberg, Klimt, and the architect Hofmann. Death, however, prevents these plans. On October 31st, three days after the death of his six-month pregnant wife, Schiele also dies from the Spanish flu. Three days thereafter, on November 3, 1918, the Austro-Hungarian Empire capitulates.

61. ***The Artist's Mother, Sleeping***, 1911.
Watercolor and lead,
45 x 31.6 cm
Graphische
Sammlung Albertina,
Vienna

62. ***Portrait of the Publisher Eduard Kosmack***, 1910.
Oil on canvas,
100 x 100 cm
Österreichische
Galerie, Vienna

63. ***Double Portrait
(Inspector in Chief
Heinrich Benesch
and his Son Otto)***,
1913. Oil on canvas,
121 x 131 cm
Neue Galerie der
Stadt Linz, Wolfgang
Gurlitt-Museum

Biography

1890: Birth of Egon Schiele in Tulln, Austria.

1890-1900: Egon devotes himself to drawing at a very young age, finding his first motifs in his native city and his surroundings.

1906: Schiele enters the Vienna Academy of Fine Arts.

1907: Meets with Gustav Klimt. Klimt influenced Schiele's first works and never ceased to encourage the young artist.

1908: Exposition in Klosterneuburg.

1909: Rebels against the teachings of his Academy professor and he writes, along with several colleagues, a list of demands asking for greater freedom of artistic expression. Because of this incident, he is forced to leave the Academy. Schiele then founds the New Art group (Neukunstgruppe) along with artists like Anton Peschka and Hans Massmann. The group will hold their first exposition at Vienna's Pisko Salon. Thanks to Klimt, Schiele is invited to the prestigious International Exhibition of Vienna.

1910: Meets with Arthur Roessler, an art critic who presents Schiele to many collectors.

1911: Works in Krumau, Bavaria. He lives with one of his models, Wally Neuzil, and the two offend the morality of the habitants of the small village. He then leaves for Neulengbach before settling down in Vienna in 1912.

1912: He exhibits in Budapest with the Neukunstgruppe and in Munich. Publication of his first lithograph. He is accused of the corruption of a minor and is sentenced to three weeks in prison between March and April, a penalty that profoundly affects him. He then records his bitterness and revolts over his punishment in his *Prison Journal*, published by Arthur Roessler in 1922. In July, he presents at Cologne's Sonderbund Exposition, one of the most outstanding events of Austrian expressionism.

64. *Mill in Ruins (Mountain Mill)*, 1915-1916. Oil on canvas, 110 x 140 cm Niederösterreichisches Landesmuseum, Vienna

1913: He is admitted into the Bund Österreichischer Künstler (a league of Austrian artists) whose president is Gustav Klimt. In March, Schiele and the other artists in the league exhibit in Budapest. He then participates in the spring exposition at the Munich Secession, at the Grosse Kunstausstellung in Berlin and at the 43rd exposition at the Vienna Secession. He also contributes his writings and drawings to the Berlin review *Die Aktion*.

1915: Marriage of Egon Schiele and Edith Harms. The effects of this lifestyle change on Schiele can be seen in his work as his eroticism became less violent. Even though he had escaped from mobilization, the medical commission returned to its decision and declared him apt for the front. He is drafted into the Austrian army. His artistic production is slowed down considerably.

1916: Schiele exhibits at the Berlin Secession and then at the Munich Secession. *Die Aktion* gives him a special issue.

1917: He returns to Vienna where he sat on the Imperial Commission. From now on, Schiele can spend his time focusing on painting. He creates the Kunsthalle, a free association of artists. He participates in an exposition at Vienna's Kaisergarten and then in various exhibitions in Amsterdam, Stockholm and Copenhagen. Schiele begins to contribute to the new Viennese movement, *Der Anbruch*.

1918: Death of Gustav Klimt on February 6th. Schiele's participation in the Viennese Secession is a success for his financial and artistic plans. A number of Viennese personalities are interested in his ever-growing body of work and success. In the fall, his wife contracts the Spanish flu and dies on October 28th. Egon Schiele follows suit and falls ill, passing away on October 31st.

65. *City Borders*,
1917-1918.
Oil on canvas,
109.5 x 139.5 cm
Neue Galerie,
Landesmuseum
Joanneum, Graz

LIST OF ILLUSTRATIONS